Other books by the author:

SUCCESS!?

HUNTER BURGAN

I HOPE YOU KNOW

HOW TO READ.

             — HUNTER

A CRITICAL COMPENDIUM HANDBOOK

Post War Science

SUCCESS!?

First Edition: July 2013

Post War Science
P.O. Box 718
Grass Valley, CA 95945
postwarscience.com

ISBN: 978-0-9894918-0-8

Library of Congress Control Number: 2013909483

TABLE OF CONTENTS

This page was intentionally left blank
until I typed this sentence and ruined it.

INTRODUCTION

Congrats! By purchasing this book you have completed the hardest step towards success.

1. Buy this book (hardest)
2. Success (next hardest)
3. Nap (easiest)

If it seems too simple that's because it is. Achieving success is much more complicated than this. I only oversimplified it so as not to scare you off. You see, motivated readers are hard to find these days. The good news is you were on the path to success before you bought this book—you just needed to lay down the cash. The bad news is you have a lot of work cut out for you. If achieving success were easy, people wouldn't have to buy a book about how to do it. Success would rank alongside other easily achievable things like eating donuts and calculating the area of a right triangle—and no one wants to buy a book about how to do *those* things![1]

---

[1] For a copy of my illustrated booklet, *How to Eat Donuts While Calculating the Area of a Right Triangle*, send $5 ppd. to the publisher's address listed on page 4.

They say you can lead a person to success, but you can't make them succeed. Truth be told, I don't know if anyone's ever said that. People usually prefer to speak metaphorically about such subjects. They say things like, "You can lead a horse to water, but you can't make it drink." What I think they're trying to say is that horses are stubborn and seldom thirsty. You don't often hear the phrase "thirsty as a stubborn horse"[2] now, do you? I would imagine that, in some cases, it might take quite a bit of coercion to get a stubborn horse to drink. Perhaps it would even necessitate leading the horse *into* the water. I don't know if horses can swim, but I would guess that even if they can, they aren't

---

[2] However, once while visiting London, I popped into a pub and ordered a drink called a "Horse's Neck". (Truthfully, I ordered a virgin "Horse's Neck" because I didn't even want to imagine what a horse's neck would have to do to lose its virginity.) The bartender winced when I said "virgin" and either asked if I was "thirsty as a stubborn horse" or let me know that it was "thirty for a southern whore"—his accent was so thick I couldn't tell which. Perhaps "thirsty as a stubborn horse" *is* an English colloquialism after all.

very good swimmers.[3] If you lead the horse deep enough, I'm sure some amount of water will eventually enter its mouth— whether the horse likes it or not. I'm not suggesting you drown the horse! That would be cruel, unnecessary and a waste of a perfectly good horse. All you need to do is strongly *suggest* that it's in the horse's best interest to take a drink of water. Make the horse an offer it can't refuse. Wait—what was I talking about? Oh yes, metaphors about success. With this book I will lead you deep into success, until only your head is sticking out and then I will strongly *suggest* it's in your best interest to succeed.

Some books are so crammed with information that the reader feels overwhelmed. Other books are so sparse and empty (like new notebooks) that the reader feels underwhelmed. I promise this book will do neither. The specific volume and density of

---

[3] It has been suggested that horses evolved from seahorses and are therefore great swimmers, but I don't buy it. In her youth, my mother was a great swimmer and all I inherited was panicky dog-paddle.

information within this book have been carefully measured and designed to be a perfect middle ground between too much and too little. This was even tested on an unsuspecting home-intruder as she entered the residence of a local family of bears. She was presented with three books on achieving success: a ridiculously dense book, a coloring book and this book. The subject read each of the books before finally settling down into a comfortable bed with the book you are holding. In her words it was "just right." So there you have it, scientific evidence that this book will leave you perfectly whelmed!

whelm |(h)welm| • verb [trans.]

> engulf, submerge, or bury (someone or something) : *a horse whelmed in a raging storm.*

WHAT IS
SUCCESS?

...and how do you spell it?

SUCCESS

YOUR
NAME
HERE

IF AT FIRST YOU *DO* SUCCEED

…set this book down.
YOU DID IT.

If not, read on.

WHAT SUCCESS ISN'T

- Success isn't easy.

- Success isn't inevitable.

- Success isn't immediate.

- Success isn't permanent.

- Success isn't at the end of every path.

- Success isn't the same thing for everyone.

- Success isn't going to come looking for *you*.

- Success isn't even aware you exist, and it certainly isn't going to give you the time of day. Success will laugh heartily if you even dare ask to peek at its $500,000 diamond Rolex, but mostly because Success just bought the watch and hasn't bothered to set it to the correct time yet.[1]

---

[1] You'd think the watch dealer would set all the watches in advance, but apparently not. Success doesn't care though, because the watch is more of a status thing anyway.

- Success isn't going to give up without a fight. Even if a criminal syndicate has kidnapped Success' grandmother and threatened to kill her if Success doesn't lose the match, Success will still go the full twelve rounds and lose by judge's decision rather than an easy knockout.

- Success isn't going to wait around for you. It's not Success' fault you overslept and missed the flight to Kathmandu. Success has no problem climbing Mount Everest without you. To be completely honest, Success isn't even sure you were physically prepared to make the trek.

- Success isn't even going to send you a postcard.[2]

I could go on and on about what success *isn't*, but you didn't buy a book about what the book isn't about, and I certainly didn't write that book.

---

[2] Believe it or not, there are no mailboxes at the top of Mt. Everest.

SUCCESS MEANS SOMETHING DIFFERENT TO DIFFERENT PEOPLE

For example: If you don't know how to read, but decided to buy this book anyway, then I successfully marketed this book to the illiterate.[3]

---

[3] If you *do* know how to read, but decided not to buy this book—consider yourself warned.

THERE'S NO *I* IN *SUCCESS*

There is a *U* in SUCCESS, but SUCCESS doesn't start with U, it starts with S, which is probably of no significance. If SUCCESS started with U it would become USCCESS, which isn't a word.

Don't let this discourage U.

SUCCESS CANNOT BE MEASURED

…by standard tools of measurement.

You must use the chart on the next page.

SUCCESS!?

Success Measurement Chart

UPON CLOSER EXAMINATION, I DISCOVERED THERE *IS* AN *I* IN *SUCᵢCESS* AFTER ALL

I sincerely apologize for any confusion this may have caused.

BUSINESS

How to Achieve Success in Business Whilst
Circumventing the Superfluously Tautological and
Pleonastically Circumlocutory Business of Success

ON SELLING YOUR SOUL
TO THE DEVIL

Despite how alluring the terms of his deal may be (and he *will* make you a very tempting offer), selling your soul to devil is never a shrewd career move. The devil is a successful soul collector and knows the market well, but he is also notorious liar and will deceive you in order to acquire your soul. Studies show that people who sell their souls on average gain a scant 2% increase in success vs. those who retain ownership of their souls.[1] Moreover, people who own their own souls live an average of 20 years longer than those without souls[2] (excluding those who received immortality) and also show a drastic 90% *decrease* in eternal servitude.[3]

---

[1] According to a real study.

[2] This is a real statistic.

[3] A known fact.

HOW TO BE A BILLIONAIRE OVERNIGHT

It's unrealistic to expect you will wake up one day as a billionaire—unless you went to sleep the night before as a billionaire. Perhaps that's the secret.[4] How do you go to sleep as a billionaire? Having a net worth of $1,000,000,000 (that's a lot of zeros!) or more is bound to be stressful. With all that money comes an enormous responsibility. It's sure to keep a billionaire awake at night! So how *do* you go to sleep as a billionaire?

Here are a few tips:

1. Maintain a regular sleep schedule.[5] Don't be afraid to nap during the day to maintain consistent bedtimes and wake-times. No one ever made a billion dollars without taking a nap.

---

[4] See page 89 for how to make a billion dollars.

[5] See pages 15 and 105 for the pitfalls of oversleeping.

2. Get a more comfortable bed. Even though a billionaire can afford the most expensive bed ever made, that golden bed isn't perhaps the most *comfortable* bed ever made.

3. Eliminate outside stimuli at bedtime. Turn off the fax machine and send the string quartet home for the night.

4. Cut down on coffee at bedtime.[6]

5. Take a hot bath or shower. This will help relax your muscles and tell your billionaire brain it's time to sleep.[7,8]

---

[6] See page 92 for specific details regarding the proper coffee intake for success.

[7] Do not fall asleep in the bathtub. Almost all billionaire drowning caused by falling asleep in the bathtub could have been avoided by reading this book. Falling asleep in the shower is rare, but also not recommended.

[8] Although a bathtub filled with coffee may prevent falling asleep and possibly drowning, it will *not* produce a relaxing effect and ultimately will defeat the purpose of the bath.

INNOVATION

Try to reinvent the wheel.

Why not? Maybe your new wheel will be so exciting that no one will remember the old wheel.

THINK *INSIDE* THE BOX

Maybe the new wheel has been inside
the box this whole time and everyone
else has been too busy with the outside to bother looking inside.

GETTING AHEAD IN TODAY'S BUSINESS WORLD

"In today's fast-paced business world it takes tenacity to get—
Oh wait, I'm sorry, you're too slow. You missed it. That was yesterday's business world. *Today's* business world takes *eleven*acity to get ahead."

— Steve Jobs[9]

---

[9] All the good Steve Jobs quotes were taken so I made this one up. However, I think Mr. Jobs had an innate understanding of how things in today's business world are intensified versions of what you have come to expect—I mean in*eleven*sified.

YESTERDAY

- TENACITY
- INTENSITY
- ATTENTION TO DETAIL
- GOOD INTENTIONS
- JUST MAKE AN ATTEMPT

TODAY

- *ELEVEN*ACITY
- IN*ELEVEN*SITY
- AT*ELEVEN*TION TO DETAIL
- GOOD IN*ELEVEN*TIONS
- JUST MAKE AN ATTEMPT[10]

---

[10] For some reason this doesn't require in*eleven*sification. I'm not sure why. Perhaps it's just a timeless business strategy.

TOMORROW*?*

- *BILLIONACITY?*
- IN*BILLION*SITY?
- AT*BILLION*TION TO DETAIL?
- GOOD IN*BILLION*TIONS?
- JUST MAKE *TWO* ATTEMPTS?

Who can say for sure!? The business world is all about "the numbers", so the future could easily end up being even more in*billion*se than economists are predicting. I wouldn't be surprised—I'd be prepared!

GO BIG OR GO HOME

If you choose to go home (which is a completely respectable choice in my opinion), at your leisure, go *big*. It will make the initial choice less about size and more about location.

Size matters, but location is everything.

SUCCESSFUL BUSINESS LUMINARIES WHOSE NAMES SHOW THEY MEAN BUSINESS

Business "Biz" Markie
(rapper, entrepreneur)

Business "Biz" Stone
(co-founder of Twitter)

Michael "Biv" Bivness
(New Edition, BBD, CEO)

Consider changing your name to
show people you mean business.

"I mean Bivness!"

NANOTECHNOLOGY IS HUGE[11]

---

[11] Find out what it's made of.

DON'T SELL YOURSELF SHORT

…unless you *are* short, then make sure to get lots of money.

SUCCESS TIP #1

If you suddenly find yourself at a complete loss and have no idea what you should be doing, that's OK! Many seasoned professionals experience this on a daily basis, even airline pilots and heart surgeons. Just don't tell anyone and hope that you figure it out before someone notices.

TWO WRONGS
DON'T MAKE A RIGHT

...they make a wrong-wrong, which is illegal in CA[12] and can be sold for a lot of money.

---

[12] May also be illegal in NY, TX, FL and IL.

BULL

BEAR

BULL vs. BEAR MARKET

Some people are still confused about the difference between a bull market and a bear market—that is to say, some people just can't tell the difference between a bull and a bear.[13] Without judgment, I offer a simple description that *I* use to differentiate the two.

A BULL has a large body, muscular legs with hooves, short hair, horns on either side of its head and a short thin tail. When angered, a bull might charge and trample or impale you.

A BEAR has a large body, thick fuzzy fur, smallish limbs and a fluff of a tail. It makes a growl or a roar when angry and might fatally maul you.

---

[13] Notwithstanding, if you see *any* type of large beast at the market, use caution and do nothing that might anger it.

RECIPE FOR SUCCESS

Success is:

50% preparation

30% perspiration

15% perturbation

8% prestidigitation

-3% math

(see the chart on opposite page)

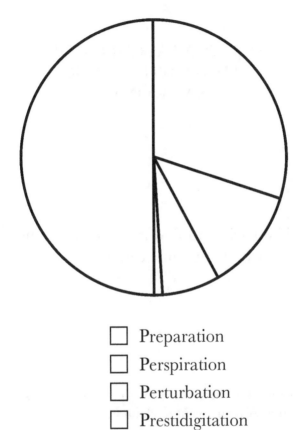

☐ Preparation
☐ Perspiration
☐ Perturbation
☐ Prestidigitation
☐ Math

Fun activity: Color the chart and
the corresponding boxes!

THERE'S A PAYCHECK OUT THERE WITH YOUR NAME ON IT

The trick is to find it before someone else with your name cashes it.

I found a check for $6 with "Larry Rogers" on it. Anyone want to claim it?

TOMORROW STARTS TODAY

If that doesn't make sense to you, call Japan and ask them what day it is.

If you're *in* Japan, call yourself. You'll get a busy signal because you're obviously too busy living in the future to answer to the past.

IT'S A DOG EAT DOG WORLD[14]

…but is it also a "human eat human" world or simply an "everybody eat dog" world? A successful business person can always tell the difference.

---

[14] Remember: You are what you eat.

MIXING BUSINESS
AND PLEASURE

If you are going to mix business and pleasure, please be forewarned that you might end up with "pusiness" or "bleasure".

IF YOU CAN'T BEAT 'EM, JOIN 'EM

...and then beat 'em in the back of the head with a big pipe when they least expect it.

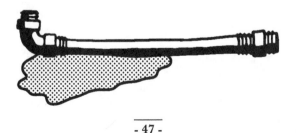

DON'T TAKE CASUAL FRIDAY
TOO SERIOUSLY

Typically everyone has given up by Friday anyway. It's "Business Thursday" that you should worry about.

KNOW WHEN IT IS TIME TO THROW IN THE TOWEL

Sometimes it's best to quit while you're ahead.

Other times it's better to gradually reduce the quality of your work until you are fired.

BIG AL

Back when I was a shiftless teenager I met a wealthy old cowboy named Big Al. One day I was roaming aimlessly through parking lots to pass the time when a shiny, red convertible pulled right in front of me. An old man in a cowboy hat and snakeskin boots stepped out of the car (it may have been a Ferrari) and walked up to me.

"Do you know who I am?!"

I shook my head.

"I'm Big Al. I own this parking lot …and the one over there too."

I shrugged.

"I'm *the* Big Al! You've never heard of me?! I could write you a check for a million dollars right now!"

I looked at Big Al's Ferrari, at the blonde woman in the passenger seat (who was much younger than Big Al), then back at Big Al and mumbled,

"Whatever, man. Maybe I don't *want* a million dollars."

Big Al must have sensed my shiftlessness because he proceeded to give me unsolicited advice about business—advice I would never forget.

BIG AL'S TWO DON'TS

1. Don't buy a fancy car.

   "Just buy yourself something that'll get you from point A to point B without breaking down or blowing up."

2. Don't get a girl pregnant.

   "You get the gist. Enough said."

BIG AL'S ONE DO

1. Get yourself some fucking
    real estate.

"I own dozens of cheap motels. You
see, people go there to fuck and they
pay me for the rooms. People fuck
and they pay *me!*"

BIG AL'S
MILLION DOLLAR DEAL

After Big Al gave me his business advice, he made a deal with me.

> "I've gotta go collect a whole buncha checks right now but here's the deal: Go out into the world and live your life, but follow my advice...and if you find that I'm wrong I want you to come back here and tell me, 'BIG AL, YOU WERE WRONG!' and I'll write you a check for a million dollars.
>
> ...but you know what? You won't be back."

And with that he jumped back into his car and drove off forever. I often think about going back and finding him but one thing always stops me—he wasn't wrong.

PERSONAL

How to Become the You that You can Become

"The journey of a thousand miles begins with a single step."

— Lao Tzu

…but the journey of a single step begins *and ends* with a single step.

Sometimes the journey of a thousand miles begins with a nap.

In the interest of not alienating those of you who use the metric system, the journey of a thousand miles is roughly equal to the journey of 1,609.34 km (kilometers).[1]

---

[1] In the further interest of not alienating those of you who are astronauts, cosmonauts, or just regular spacemen; the journey of a thousand miles is roughly equal to the journey of 0.00000000017011142836059 ly (light years) or for the astrophysicists, roughly 0.0000000000052155287051489 pc (parsecs).

GIVE A MAN A FISH
AND HE EATS FOR A DAY

...unless he's a vegetarian, in which case he will take the fish to town and trade it for three magic beans. You know the rest.

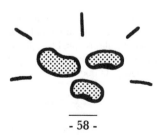

GIVE A MAN A MICROWAVE
AND HE EATS FOR A DAY

Teach a man to emit microwaves from his eyes and he will rule the world with violence and fear.

AN OLD RECIPE FOR SUCCESS

You can only have two:

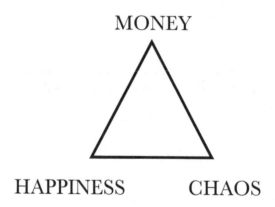

MONEY

HAPPINESS   CHAOS

Choose wisely.

GIVE A MAN A MICROWAVE
AND HE EATS FOR A DAY

Teach a man to emit microwaves from his eyes and he will rule the world with violence and fear.

AN OLD RECIPE FOR SUCCESS

You can only have two:

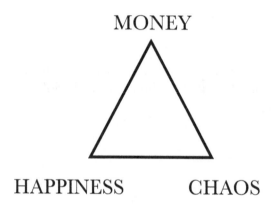

MONEY

HAPPINESS   CHAOS

Choose wisely.

SUCCESS TIP #2

Having trouble getting out of bed in the morning? Try putting snakes under your bed sheets. Not only will it motivate you to leave the bed as soon as you become conscious, but you'll also create the "snakes under the bed sheets" look that is so popular these days.

YOUR DREAMS AREN'T GOING TO FOLLOW THEMSELVES

That would be too easy.[2]

---

[2] If for some reason your dreams start following *you* and it becomes a problem, it might be a good idea to get a restraining order against them—just for now, until you find some dreams that aren't creepy stalkers.

HOW TO TURN YOUR WILDEST DREAMS INTO REALITY

1. Dream something crazy.
2. Wake up and plan a way to do it.
3. Do it.
4. Go back to sleep.
5. Repeat until you run out of money or die.

"All our wildest dreams can come true, if we have the money to pursue them."

— Walt Disney[3]

---

[3] Maybe I just made that up.

ON FOLLOWING YOUR DREAMS

I know you're eager to dive right in and immediately make all your dreams come true, but some of them may not be the type of dreams you should turn into reality. It's important to know which of your dreams you should follow and which you should simply try to forget.

One time I had a dream that I was speeding along a desert highway when I noticed a colossal wall of earth moving towards me on the horizon. It was an apocalyptic "tidal wave" of dirt; at least a mile high and I knew that it would be impossible to escape.

This is not the type of dream I would try to follow.

Another time I dreamt that I ran into John Cleese at a hotel in Hawaii. He was disguised as an elevator operator and gave me £20 to keep his identity a secret. Now *this* is exactly the type of dream I would try to follow. It has everything I look for in a dream: great characters, exotic locations, mystery, intrigue and cash.[4]

---

[4] If you are traveling abroad, you will likely need to exchange currency at some point. International airports are a convenient place to exchange your money and they will usually give you a pretty good rate. If you receive foreign currency in a dream, it's a smart idea to exchange it right away since you never know when you might wake up. If an airport isn't close by, a hotel or bank will also do the trick. For me, hotels are an obvious choice for my mid-slumber currency conversion since I often dream of staying in really nice hotels.

"Please don't tell anyone!"

SEVEN STEPS TO DAILY SUCCESS

1. Set extremely low standards. Make sure your goals are easy to achieve.

2. If something doesn't turn out as planned, retroactively state that the outcome was your intention all along. You just needed to keep it a secret until everything was finished.

3. Hang out with only the most successful people—and please tell them about this book.

4. Be an unstoppable force.[5] Should you encounter an immovable object, do not attempt to move it. Don't try

---

[5] Another option you can't refuse: An irresistible force.

to be a hero, simply go around the object. You don't want to end up stuck in a paradox.

5. Don't be afraid to ask for help. This will be especially important when you are bleeding or on fire.

6. Choose only the path that leads to your future. Once you've reached the future, gather as much information about lottery numbers as you can, then take the path back to the present.

7. Don't be afraid of failure, rejection or death. They happen to even the most successful people. Did you remember to tell them about this book?

STRESSED SPELLED BACKWARDS IS DESSERTS

This could come in handy if you're ever in a spelling bee.

SUCCESS SPELLED
BACKWARDS IS SSECCUS

Don't bother learning to spell words backwards unless you do a lot of reading with a mirror.[6]

---

[6] A special backwards edition of this book is coming soon!

THE EARLY BIRD
GETS THE WORM

...but think about it—do you really want a gross worm?!

What would you even do with a worm?!

THE EARLY WORM
GETS EATEN

A recent study[7] showed that worms who habitually sleep late have much longer life expectancies than worms who consider themselves early risers.

---

[7] Why do scientists know so much about the sleep patterns of worms? It's 2013—are you really surprised?

FIVE WORDS TO LIVE BY

FLATTERY WILL GET YOU SOMEWHERE

…but you might have to call a cab to get home.

WHERE DO YOU SEE YOURSELF IN TEN YEARS?

I usually answer this question by saying, "a mirror" because that's where I see myself the most. However, it's difficult to speculate how mirror technology will advance over the next ten years.

WALK A MILE IN
ANOTHER MAN'S SHOES

If you've stolen a man's shoes, one mile is a sufficient head start, especially if he doesn't immediately notice his shoes are gone.[8]

---

[8] If he's a short tempered man or prone to violent rage, you may want to *run* a mile in his shoes.

THE ROAD TO SUCCESS IS PAVED WITH ASPHALT, LIKE MOST ROADS

What did you expect?

Something less concrete?

OTHER

Sometimes the nature of your success
is neither business nor personal.

SOMETIMES YOU CAN'T SEE THE FOREST *OR* THE TREES

…because it's really dark.

SUCCESS, ARKANSAS

Success is a town in Clay County, Arkansas. According to the United States Census Bureau, the population is a scant 147. Success is very difficult, if not impossible to find.[1] Many people spend their whole lives searching for it, like a modern-day El Dorado or Shangri-La. One of the reasons Success is so elusive is its small size. Success has a total area of 0.2 mi² (0.6 km²), meaning it would take about 5 minutes to walk the entire width of town.

---

[1] If you're having trouble finding Success, it is located here: 36°27′16″N 90°43′23″W

AS ONE DOOR CLOSES, ANOTHER ONE OPENS

It's called an air lock.

GENIES

One of the fastest ways to enjoy the spoils of success without any hard work is to find a lamp[2] with a genie inside. Standard genie protocol allows them to grant three wishes. You can wish for almost anything, but some genies have specific provisions prohibiting wishing for additional wishes.[3]

WARNING: Genies are notorious jerks, so be careful when dealing with them. They would love nothing more than to trick you and leave you in a less fortuitous position than you started. Often the wishes they grant come with an enormous price. Genies have even been known to trap unsuspecting

---

[2] Genies can also be found in old bottles.

[3] A monkey's paw will also occasionally grant wishes to the bearer, but this is rare and does not apply to all monkey's paws. Most of the time your wishes will *not* be granted and you will also have an angry monkey on your hands.

people inside the very lamps from which they themselves were freed. Carefully consider your wishes (including how they're worded) in advance.

Example: You should learn the difference between omnipotent and impotent *before* you ask the genie to grant your wish.

BONUS: GENIE JOKES[4]

Question: Why did the genie cross the road?

Answer: Why did the genie do *anything?!* You wish you knew, but then you just wasted one wish!

Question: What do you get when you cross a genie with—STOP RIGHT THERE—For your own safety and the safety of those you love, *never* cross a genie.

---

[4] You should never, under any circumstances whatsoever, tell these jokes when a genie is present. Also, don't mention that you read them in this book.

THE NEXT TIME YOU'RE AN HOUR LATE USE THE "DAYLIGHT SAVINGS EXCUSE"

"You guys still use daylight savings?!
I haven't used that since I was a kid!"[5]

---

[5] This excuse will not work as well if you are still a kid.

UNOBEJCTIONABLE

I have nothing against this word.

"You cannot plow a field by turning it over in your mind."

— Author Unknown

"…unless it's a mind field."

— Hunter Burgan

HOW TO MAKE
A BILLION DOLLARS

The economy of the modern world is in a constant state of flux. The real value of paper money is questionable at best. To make matters worse, it has become increasingly difficult to make money—or has it? Here's an easy way to make a billion dollars.

Things you will need:

- A million dollar bill
- A black marker

1. Using the marker, write a capital letter *B* over each of the *M*s on both sides of the bill. Take care to only do this to the *M*s that appear in the word *MILLION* and not words like *AMERICA*. *ABERICA* is not a real place and you will have just wasted a million dollars.

2. Take the bill to the corner store and use it to buy a pack of gum or some tic tac®s. The store clerk may ask you if you have any smaller bills. Just apologize and say something like, "No, I just got paid today."

3. Put the change into the suitcases you brought with you and return home to celebrate with your tic tac®s. You just made a billion dollars![6]

---

[6] I was initially going to include this in the *BUSINESS* section of this book, but I decided that this type of activity isn't a sound business decision. You can really only do this once or twice before arousing suspicion. Also, since this might be illegal (to be honest, I haven't checked the specific laws regarding this type of activity in every country) you're advised to proceed with caution. I hereby take no responsibility for anything that happens if you decide to violate any laws or local ordinances.

THERE'S NO *TEAM* IN *WORK*

There's simply a lone *work*, which is exactly what you need to do sometimes to achieve success—work alone, while everyone else is outside playing.

SUCCESS TIP #3

Switch from a large coffee to a small coffee.[7] You probably don't need all the extra caffeine and you will appear to be more in control of your habits—and your life! Plus, you can always get a refill.

---

[7] If you are already drinking a small coffee, switch to a large. You could probably use the extra caffeine. If you don't drink coffee at all, switch to a medium.

NEVER LET 'EM
SEE YOU SWEAT

Furthermore, never let 'em see *any* fluids leave your body. It shows weakness and you are not weak. As far as they know, your body is watertight.

SUCCESS!?

SUCCESS, THE PRISON SHIP

Success was a large wooden ship built in 1840 and used as an Australian prison ship. *Success* carried hundreds of men, handcuffed or shackled in irons. These men were cruelly tortured (often flogged) and many of them died as a result. Years later, *Success* would become a stationary prison hulk.[8] It is said that not a single person ever successfully escaped from *Success*. Needless to say, this is not the kind of success you should aspire to.

---

[8] Even later, in 1890, *Success* would become a museum, traveling around the world drawing attention to the atrocity and barbarity that took place during the colonial convict era. *Success* was awaiting dismantlement in Lake Erie when vandals finally destroyed it on July 4th, 1946. Poetic justice?

ONE MAN'S TREASURE IS
ANOTHER MAN'S TRASH

If you're that first man, you should make
sure another man isn't throwing away your
treasure!

WINNING AND LOSING

Winning isn't *everything*—there's also losing.

WINNERS DIDN'T START
OUT AS WINNERS

...they started out as babies. Losers also started out as babies though, so if you're a baby right now you've got at least a 50/50 chance of being a winner. Those are decent odds, baby.

PROFIT AND LOSS

When I was seven years old I learned a valuable lesson about profit and loss. It was the day after Halloween and I had returned to school with a small sack of candy from the night before.[1] Upon examining my candy I noticed that the wrapper to my prized 3 MUSKETEERS® bar had a small hole in it. I remembered all the horrible things I had seen on TV about homicidal strangers putting razor blades, needles and poison into unsuspecting trick-or-treaters' sacks. It was true! I had a poisoned 3 MUSKETEERS® in my possession! I was sorely disappointed since it was my favorite candy and I couldn't even eat it without dying! I told an acquaintance (for the purpose of this story we'll call

---

[1] As a child I often participated in a ritual known as Trick-or-Treating, which may have Pagan origins. I'm not sure. I was just in it for the candy.

him Mike[2]) about my poisoned candy and he offered to trade me for one of his candies. "Are you crazy? It's poisoned!" I reminded him. He didn't seem to care! I made a counter offer: my poisoned 3 MUSKETEERS® for not one, but *two* of his candies. Mike agreed and we made the trade.

PROFIT!

I then watched Mike slowly enjoy the 3 MUSKETEERS® bar without convulsing, bleeding from the mouth or puking his guts out. It wasn't poisoned after all! I was glad Mike was all right, but slightly bothered that I had traded away my favorite candy bar. I still felt I had made a profitable exchange though: two for one. I opened up my two new candies to find, to my chagrin, that they were both licorice—I hate licorice! I would rather puke my guts out than eat licorice!

LOSS!

---

[2] I decided to call him Mike because that was his real name and he liked being called that. We remained acquainted through third grade but ultimately drifted apart by junior high.

IT'S NOT WHETHER YOU WIN OR LOSE, IT'S HOW YOU PLAY THE GAME

Did you buy those lottery tickets with style and panache? Did you allow the orange ghost[3] to kill *Ms. Pac-Man* with grace and courage?

---

[3] The orange ghost in *Ms. Pac-Man* is named Sue. In the original *Pac-Man*, the orange ghost is named Clyde. Blinky, Pinky and Inky appear in both games, leading me to believe that Clyde made some smart investments early in his career and doesn't need to work two jobs to put food on the table like the other ghosts. He was also thoughtful enough to get his sister a job.

LIFE HAS ITS UPS AND DOWNS
JUST LIKE *SNAKES & LADDERS*

The ladders allow you to climb higher towards success and the snakes force you to slide down their scaly backs to meet your doom.

THE 4 *N*s OF WI*NN*I*NN*G

1. Networking. Make connections with others in your field.

2. Never stop trying. Persisence isn't a word, but *persistence* is one of the keys to success.

3. Networking again. Make connections with some more people—maybe this time, for a change, try looking for people that *don't* hang out in that weird cornfield where you spend so much of your time.

4. Nap. Take a nap. You've earned it.

THE 1 *OS* AND 1 *G* OF LO*S*ING

1. Over-Sleeping. Keep your mid-day snoozing to a minimum, Rip Van Winkle. A short nap on the job is a great way to recharge, but if you over-sleep you may be putting your life (as well as the lives of others) at risk.[4]

1. Gambling. The fastest way to lose your hard-earned cash is gambling. Some might argue that gambling is also the fastest way to *win* hard-earned cash, but that's false. Any money you won would not technically be hard-earned.[5]

---

[4] This includes, but is not limited to the following professions: bus drivers, deep-sea divers, carnival knife throwers, railroad track inspectors, human cannonballs, lion tamers and the people who defuse nuclear warheads.

[5] Plus, I bet you'd throw it all away on silly quarter slots.

"There is no success without suc and cess."

— Hunter Burgan[6]

---

[6] Nobody enjoys suckin' cess, but it pays off in the end.

DRAWING

It's not whether you win or lose, but how you draw.

HOW TO DRAW UP A
HIGH SCHOOL DIPLOMA

Is a high school diploma the one thing missing from your resume? If your lack of a high school diploma is keeping you from achieving the success you think you deserve, why not draw one up?[1]

Here's how!

The easiest way:

1. Borrow someone else's diploma.

2. Scan it into a computer.

3. Replace their name with your own.

4. Print it out.

5. Frame it and put it on the wall.

---

[1] For entertainment purposes only, right?

If this is too easy or you simply don't have access to a computer, you can always do it by hand:

1. Borrow someone else's diploma.

2. Carefully trace the document using a light table or tracing paper. Don't forget to write your name on it!

3. Use gold foil[2] to replicate any official seals.

4. Frame it and put it on the wall.

Not everyone is able to successfully complete his or her studies while in high school. Similarly, not everyone will be able to successfully draw up his or her own diploma. If drawing up documents is not your forte, you can always "earn" your diploma the old fashioned way, in high school!

---

[2] Gold foil can be found at most art supply stores and is a fairly inexpensive way to make your diploma look official. While you're there, why not pick up some graduation themed stickers for your scrapbook? You've earned 'em!

HOW TO SUCCESSFULLY SLEEP THROUGH A LECTURE
(WITHOUT DRAWING UNNECESSARY ATTENTION TO YOURSELF)

How many times have you had to endure a painfully boring lecture because you simply had no way of inconspicuously sleeping through it? Here's a simple way to take a quick nap without getting caught:

1. Draw eyeballs on your eyelids.

2. Nap.[3]

---

[3] Don't forget to set an alarm to wake you before the end of the lecture!

BEYOND SUCCESS

For those who dare to dream the undreamable dream
and achieve the unachievable achievements—
now what?!

SIX POPULAR
MONOGRAM STYLES

Successful people like to have their initials embroidered on things like robes, handkerchiefs, shirt cuffs and towels to let others know who owns them. In your case that would be you! But which style monogram will you choose? Here are six popular styles:

Fancy

Angular

Bold Serif
(larger middle initial)

Unapologetically Fancy
(almost illegible)

Traditional Serif

Heavy Metal

IDEAL NAPPING LOCATIONS

After achieving success you will want to celebrate with a well-deserved nap. Here are a
few select places to enjoy a quick snooze:

- On the beach
- Under a big oak tree
- On a park bench by a
  playground
- On a mattress under a bridge
- Behind a refuse container in a
  metropolitan alleyway[1]
- Under the bushes behind a
  supermarket
- In the soft golden sunlight that
  shines through the broken
  window of an abandoned
  building

---

[1] This can also be a good place to find a low-calorie snack.

ON VISITING YOUR ENEMY'S GRAVE

Although "Forgive and Forget" is always the best policy, sometimes achieving success requires crushing your enemies. Later, when it's convenient, you should visit their graves to show that you forgive them for all the awful things they did to you over the years, and even though success unquestionably necessitated crushing them without mercy, it certainly wasn't done without a tinge of remorse. It probably seems like only yesterday when they muttered the overused phrase, "This town ain't big enough for the both of us," to which you replied, "*Isn't.* This town *isn't* big enough for the both of us."

MEETING THE NEW YOU

Success has a way of changing people. Once you become successful it may take you some time to become accustomed to the new you. You may even begin to treat yourself like a celebrity, and when you catch a glimpse of yourself in the mirror, you say,

> "Who's that successful guy? Oh look, it's me."

Then you suddenly catch yourself staring at yourself in the mirror, so you try to play it off and quickly look away—before you're able to snap a photo of yourself. But you're not fast enough because you caught yourself taking a picture. Then you realize that you took a picture of yourself *taking a picture* of yourself, and it's a little bit awkward so you decide to take a shot in the dark and say what you've been thinking.

> "I love your work. I'm one of your biggest fans."

And as the words leave your mouth you realize that your personal hero is saying the same thing back to you. You have a mutual appreciation for each other—and you could not have wished for a better interaction with a personal hero. Then you decide to take it one step further. Why not?

> "I would love to hang out with you for a day…do what *you* do…see what it's like to live in your world."

Then comes the biggest shock. Both you and your hero had the same idea! Your eyes lock as you both simultaneously exclaim,

> "Yes! It would be an honor!"

What a dream come true! This is the best day of your life!

SPEND EVERY DAY AS IF YOU ARE TAGGING ALONG WITH A SUCCESSFUL VERSION OF YOURSELF

DEAR HUNTER

Letters to the Author[1]

---

[1] Since, as logic would dictate, this book is unpublished at the time of writing; I have yet to receive a single letter. Therefore this section is completely hypothetical.

Dear Hunter,

Sometimes I feel like I'm going nowhere. How do I know if the path that I'm currently on leads to success?

Signed,

Richard Branson[2]

Dear Mr. Branson,

Find a small child, preferably one with a bicycle and offer this child one dollar to ride to the end of your path and return with a detailed description of what he or she found there.

Dear Hunter,

I bought a home just before the "subprime mortgage crisis" and now I'm underwater with my mortgage. To make matters worse, my partner and I separated last month,

---

[2] I don't think this is *the* Sir Richard Branson, founder and chairman of Virgin Group, but then again there was no return address on the envelope.

leaving me barely able to make my monthly payment. I feel like I'm stuck between a rock and a hard place. What do I do?

Desperately seeking success,

Susan

Dear Susan,

Nobody enjoys being stuck between a rock and a hard place, but it's a great place to learn important life lessons. Conversely, most people *do* enjoy being stuck between a pillow and a soft place because it's a great place to take a nap. Give it time and eventually the rock will erode enough for you to wiggle out.[3] Water could also play an important part in the erosion process, so if you're underwater as you mentioned, the rock may erode even faster. Alternately, if you are

---

[3] Studies suggest that granite (which has an average density of 2650 k/m³) erodes at an average rate of somewhere between ~1 to 30 meters every million years, depending on specific climactic and tectonic environment. I imagine geologists will have more specific information by the year 1,000,000. In the meantime, let's hope *your* rock is less dense than granite—otherwise you may be stuck for a bit!

certain you can get free by cutting your arm off, you may want to consider doing so—but only as a last resort. Although cutting one's arm off is not always irreversible, it is a desperate final act that should not be taken lightly.

Dear Hunter,

I am a 74 year old man serving back-to-back sentences for forgery (counterfeiting a billion dollar bill) and assault with a deadly weapon (I beat someone in the back of the head with a big pipe). By the time I'm released I will be well into my 80s. Will it still be possible for me to achieve success as a model?

> Cautiously optimistic,
>
> Col. Mustard

Dear Mr. Mustard,

There's been recent growth in the senior modeling industry. With hard work and the right representation, there's no limit to what you can achieve.

THE ONE BIG SECRET TO SUCCESS

...can be found on the next page.

THE ONE BIG SECRET
TO SUCCESS

If you skipped ahead to this page hoping you'd find the one big secret to success, then you're in luck—you found it![1] However, your method is all wrong. Success isn't a page you can simply skip to at the end of a book. It's not a destination, it's a journey; the journey of a thousand miles—but if you had read this book from the beginning you'd already know that.

---

[1] It's written at the top of the page.

ABOUT THE AUTHOR

Hunter Burgan is a successful musician, author, speaker, listener and self-made thousandaire. He lives in a small shack in Los Angeles and prefers his coffee small.

www.hunterburgan.com

@TranquilMammoth